How

MW01094551

7 Easy Steps to Master Goal Setting, Goal Planning, Smart Goals, Motivational Psychology & Achieving Goals

Miles Toole

More by Miles Toole

Discover all books from the Personal Productivity Series by
Miles Toole at:

bit.ly/miles-toole

Book 1: *How to Be Productive*

Book 2: *How to Manage Time*

Book 3: *How to Be Organized*

Book 4: *How to Stay Focused*

Book 5: *How to Set Goals*

Book 6: *How to Stop Procrastinating*

Book 7: *How to Change Habits*

Book 8: *How to Stay Motivated*

Themed book bundles available at discounted prices:

bit.ly/miles-toole

Copyright

Table of Contents

Introduction

Welcome to *"How to Set Goals"*. Everyone will tell you how goal setting is an important thing for all aspects of your life. And I think you already know that, but what you do not know is how you can set goals in your life, and that is something we are going to discuss in this guide. Once you do that, your productivity levels will rise and so will your sense of self-confidence. When you have a compelling and clear goal in front of your eyes, that will promote actionable behavior and will also increase your focus. You will learn that you should not settle for just anything that comes your way but work to get the best.

Whenever you have a goal, all your focus and effort will automatically go in that direction. And most importantly, goals will help you build your character. You will start understanding what you want in life and what is truly important for you. Also, if you think that setting goals is a boring process, then your thoughts are about to change, and by the time you reach the end of this guide, you will not only have your own goals but you will also be working towards them. The satisfaction derived from this cannot be replaced by anything else.

Chapter 1: Step 1 – Write Down Your Goals

If you think that you do not have goals, then you are wrong because everyone has them. What you need to do is simply figure them out. No matter how small or big it is, if you want to achieve something in life, then that is definitely one of your goals. But achieving goals and setting goals are two completely different things. And I know that some of you might be thinking that writing your goals down is probably the most clichéd thing you have heard but trust me, I am saying this from personal experience, that writing down your goals definitely helps a lot.

There was a study conducted by Dr. Gail Matthews to show that writing down your goals is actually fruitful. The study included a total of 270 participants, and the results showed that 42% of them were able to achieve their respective goals because they wrote them down. When you write your goals, you become more clear-headed on what you want and so it acts as a motivator for your actions. You know exactly what you want to accomplish and so, you move towards it without any confusion at all. When you are putting those goals on paper, you are actually promoting yourself to strategize to make those dreams come true. You will also be asking yourself how much you have progressed so far and the spend time brainstorming what your plan of action should be.

And, you don't have to take my word for this because there are some interesting experiments backing all these claims of writing down your goals. It was found by a Harvard Business Study that among the students enrolled in MBA, only 3% were able to graduate because their goals were clearly written and then even got better job packages where they earned way better than the other 97% students.

But there is a method of writing down your goals as well. Goal planning is an art, and you have to do it the right way to reap the results. So, here are some of the tips that you should follow if you want to get the benefit from writing down your goals.

Define Your Goals

Now, I know you might be thinking that it is not a difficult task to define your goals because all you have to do is explain what you want but it is not that much easy as well. Do you know why? Everyone has a busy routine to follow, and while doing all of that people often forget what they really had in mind. Circumstances are what guides most people around you but if you don't want to be someone like that, then you have to take your life in your own hands and shape your life the way you want, keeping your goals in mind. If you ask yourself who is happier – whether it is the person who chases his/her goals or the person who gets dictated by his/her circumstances, then I am sure the answer will be the former one. But ask yourself in which category you fall and which category you want to make yourself fall in.

If you are going through this chapter, then I think you are currently in the latter category but want to be in the former one, and that can be done. Start by analyzing the situation that you are in. For that, you have to take some time out, sit down and really think. You have to reflect on your life and you have to sit in a quiet place where no one is going to disturb you. Consider all the angles and then figure out what your situation is and once you are down, note down everything that you feel and see.

Start Looking at the Bigger Picture

When you are writing down your goals, you should be picturing yourself as to what you want to achieve next year or even five or six years down the lane. In simpler words, I am asking you to think about what your long-term goals are. You do not have to think about how you are going to achieve these goals or any of the details related to that. All I am asking you to, is to envision yourself in that position. Dream about it and think whether you truly want it.

It can be a professional goal or even a personal one – it doesn't really matter. You simply have to remove the rein on your heart and let it speak. It can be something like setting up your own company five years down the lane, or it can also be having your own children and getting married. Or, it can be that you want to climb a mountain or you want to get promoted to a higher position which involves greater pay. Or, you might even want to take a gap year to travel the world. There is no end to the goals that a person can have and so you must not stop yourself from dreaming and start looking at what the bigger picture looks like. Also, no matter how far-fetched your dream looks to you now, you should definitely write it down.

When your goals have already been articulated, feel them, and visualize them. You can also make a vision board for yourself. I know that it sounds like school-level craftwork, but a vision board can really emanate a positive vibe and make you work towards it. Your brain cells get activated and they start cementing all these goals strongly in your mind. Since this is a creative process, it will ensure that your rational thinking does not stop you from seeing what you can do. Also, while you are doing this, don't ever stress too much about creating something perfect. Do whatever you enjoy doing in the way that you like and not in a way as if you have to create a masterpiece.

Don't Forget to Look at the Smaller Picture

Now, once you have figured out your bigger picture, it is time that you start filling in the gaps that are present in between, that is, the time from now to your actual goal. So, start thinking about what the first step could be. For example, if your goal is to set up your company, then you need to start by figuring out a niche in which you are going to start the company. If you want to get married, then you either have to propose your loved one for marriage, or you should get into online dating apps or ask your friends to set you up with someone. If you want to achieve your goal weight or body, then start by visiting a nutritionist and figure out your diet plan. Remember that nothing happens on its own. You have to work towards it to make it happen and that involves taking the first step.

If you think that you will have to get enrolled for some courses in order to make your dream come true, then do it. If you see that the basic thing that is required for your goal to be met is already present with you, then start figuring out the next step. You have to take time off and map out all your steps and then write them down.

Understand Your Goals

If you want to master the art of goal setting, you also have to understand each and every goal that you are writing down. If you do not truly understand the things you want, you will go off the track very easily, and you will not be feeling motivated to achieve anything. When someone wants to succeed in something, they also have to find in themselves the tenacity of doing so. So, start interrogating yourself regarding each and every goal. Ask yourself why you want to achieve that particular goal and if there are any other doors that will open up for you when you achieve it.

You should also ask yourself about how you will feel when you achieve the goal. Ask yourself why you want to achieve that goal now and not anytime else. If you are having trouble doing this exercise, then you can try it in a reverse manner as well – ask yourself what will happen if you fail to achieve the goal.

Stick to Positive Language Only

Whenever you are practicing the goal setting exercise, don't use any negative words. You should always view everything in a positive light. If you are into a process of negative goal setting, then the process is going all wrong. It will soon become a toxic cycle. So, let me give you a few examples to help you understand his better –

- If you are not finding the right person to date, then you should not say – 'Stop fooling around with losers.' This promotes a negative vibe. So, you must reframe it and say something like – 'Find yourself a partner who will be supportive, loving, and successful.'

- Similarly, if you are not happy with the job you are currently doing, don't say 'Resign from your dead-end job.' Reframe it into 'Start looking for a job that will align with your passions and your skills.'

Changing the language from negative to positive can have a great impact on how you take your goal to be. If you use negative language, you might feel depressed as if you are criticizing your present self. But when you use positive language, you will automatically feel excited about the new endeavor ahead. You will be more determined than ever to go past any hurdle that comes your way and achieve your goals.

Chapter 2: Step 2 – Set Realistic Goals

There is motivational psychology that works behind setting realistic goals. When we are talking about goals, it is pretty easy to become lost in them and start dreaming of things that are unrealistic. So, if you want goals to be achievable, you have to practice realistic goal setting which means that you have to stop fantasizing about things that are too far-fetched, and instead of wasting your time behind them, you have to start spending your time planning out those goals which are realistic.

Did you know that one of the major reasons why people fail at achieving their goals is because they fail to take all the steps that are necessary for fulfilling it or they are not able to take the rightful measures in time and lastly, they struggle with progress because what they are trying to achieve is not possible in reality? And unrealistic goal setting goes on and on like a vicious cycle, and every time you are not able to achieve something, you will feel bad about it and set another goal which might be too difficult for you to achieve then. So, in this chapter, I am going to tell you why it is so important for you to set goals that are realistic and what you can do to set them.

Importance of Realistic Goals

Many people ask me why they should start setting realistic goals and wouldn't it reduce their potential to achieve bigger things in life? Well, let me clear this out for you once and for all. This is nothing but a false assumption. When you have high expectations, you are putting all your effort and self-esteem into it and you already have an image conjured inside your head. But what happens when you fail to meet those standards that you have set for yourself? What happens when the reality does not match with the conjured image? You immediately start loathing yourself and have all kinds of negative vibes which, in turn, hampers your self-worth and you ultimately see yourself as a complete and utter failure.

But when your goals are realistic, none of this happens because you are not attached to any such high expectations, and you are simply giving your best and enjoying what you do. Realistic expectations mean that you are no longer focused on what might happen and what won't. You become more focused on things that you can control and thus, increase your performance. The outside factors and incidences occurring around you cannot be controlled by you but you can definitely practice full control of what is happening inside of you. Thus, your thought processes are no longer messed with expectations and you are able to let go of the 'all-or-none' attitude.

So, here are some of the benefits of realistic goal setting:

Helps You Take One Step at a Time

When I told you in the previous chapter that you should not settle for less, by that, I did not mean that you should think unrealistically. If you set goals that are unrealistic and give in to the idea of having grandiose dreams, then it might just backfire. You have to think big (there is no denying that) but thinking big does not mean that your feet have to come off the ground. You still have to remain in your reality. For example, if you think that you want to earn $5,000 a month, then that is a good goal but it will be unrealistic for you if you are currently not earning anything from your online business.

So, when your goal is to earn $5,000, and in that month, you are able to earn only $500, it is going to affect your self-esteem and you are going to feel so bad that you might just back off from the whole endeavor. That is why you have to judge the circumstance that you are in and then set a goal of say $1000 a month (which is achievable). You simply have to make small milestones like this in order to reach your ultimate goal.

Each year in your life doesn't have to be about a newer and more intensive competition. You have to relax a bit and stop trying to do everything at the same time. If you think that way, there are no ends to how high a standard can rise. There will be endless growth in any industry but sometimes, you simply have to take a break and take off the pressure from your shoulders.

When people set goals that are extraordinary, there is a lot that goes beyond it to make it successful and this, eventually, leads to a 'crash-and-burn' situation where you work so intensively towards something for the first few days or weeks that you burn out later on and cannot carry on with it anymore. This results in people quitting because they are too exhausted, and it is a very toxic situation to handle.

But when your goals are realistic, you can take them one step at a time, and your ultimate goal will automatically seem way more achievable and easier. Moreover, when you set goals that are realistic, you realize that goal planning is not always about the bigger things. Sometimes, doing small and easier things add up and help to make your ultimate dream come true while making the process easier at the same time. And so, when you realize this, you will be motivated and come up with a better plan.

No More Unreasonable Expectations to Deal With

When things do not go as planned, most people start beating themselves up, and they treat themselves in a very harsh manner. It is in human nature to feel shame and guilt whenever something doesn't happen the way it should have. And this is where self-hatred is born. The only solution out of this is to change your state of mind. You cannot go on with negative feelings and that is where motivational psychology comes in. When you let go of the unreasonable expectations, you have nothing to worry about and no standard to keep up with. You can simply give your best and then wait for the results. There are no high expectations forcing you to work more than you can handle.

You Will Get Small Yet Continuous Wins

Remember how I said that you should have milestones leading up to your ultimate goal. Well, that is what these small wins are. When you set expectations keeping reality in mind, you gather small goals that add up to your big goal, and whenever you meet any of these small goals, you are going to get a boost of confidence. The process becomes much more meaningful. Whenever you are adding small wins to your crown, you are becoming more motivated to achieve the next goal as well and in this way, you go on winning continuously. Isn't this much better than setting unrealistic goals and failing every time only to lose your self-worth and self-confidence all over again?

How to Set Realistic Goals?

Now that you know why I am asking you to set realistic goals, it is time to learn how you can do that.

Assess Your Commitment

When you have figured out what your realistic goals are, it is time you think about whether you are truly committed to your goals or not? Do you have what is required to follow through your goals? Having the right goals and the right strategy will never be enough if you are not ready to follow them. Also, if you are truly passionate about your goals, you will not have to think twice before committing to them. It should come naturally to you. Also, if your list is crammed up with too many goals, then you should remove some of them. You don't have to simply omit them, but keep them for a later time when you have finished what you already have on your plate. When you try to do too many things at a time, you might not feel like doing any of them at all.

Be Very Specific

When you are writing your goals down, be very specific about them. Write every detail associated with the goal. When you go into the details associated with a goal, it will also help you realized whether the goal is realistic or not. You can also do some of your own research and learn about the things that are involved in the process. Some of the things that you should try to learn about are what will be required to fulfill the goal, how expensive it can be, or how much effort it will need.

Take Your Limitations into Account

Realistic goal planning is incomplete if you don't take stock of your limitations. There is nothing to be shy about because every single person on this earth has some kind of limitation or the other. And these are the barriers that you will have to encounter while trying to achieve your goal.

Some people find it difficult to identify what their limitations are. Well, they can come in many forms. They can be physical or even monetary. Some of the limitations can be overcome very easily while some are too difficult and so you might even have to reframe or revise your goals. To get a clearer picture, you should write your limitations on a piece of paper and then see the goals that you had written down previously. See how much of a barrier your limitations can pose in the path of achieving your goals.

You should not forget the external obstacles because they are a form of limitation too. For example, if you want to get admitted to your dream school, then you have to assess what are the requirements and eligibility criteria and whether you meet all of them. Sometimes, the fees may be too high for you to afford it. If you are not meeting the eligibility criteria, then it can be difficult to get into that school and sometimes even impossible. But if the problem is money, then that can be sorted out in different ways like a scholarship or a student loan.

Chapter 3: Step 3 – Learn to Be Accountable

I think every one of us can talk for endless hours when it comes to our dreams and aspirations. But, there are so many people who keep on procrastinating and do not perform anything to turn their dreams into reality. Your idea or plan might be the best, and you might even have all the talent and ambition required to achieve the goals but none of that is going to happen until and unless you take the first step. But if you start holding yourself accountable, then this problem can be solved. You will become better at goal planning if you are accountable for what you do. You will be walking steadily towards achieving goals if you learn how to hold yourself accountable. It will also help you in enhancing your performance and also reduce your stress.

Accountability is one of those factors that separates successful people from mediocre. That is why so many people who are trying to adopt a healthier lifestyle are also advised to get into an accountability program because that keeps them going and keeps them motivated to continue their new lifestyle.

Benefits of Accountability

Before we move on to the steps that you can take to be accountable, let me give you a brief intro into the benefits that accountability can bring into your life and help in effective goal setting.

- ***Boost Your Performance*** – One of the very first ways in which accountability is going to benefit you is that you will be able to carry out all your work with confidence. If you are taking the help of a coach for this, then you will also know that your plan has been monitored by an expert and someone who really knows this stuff.

- ***Helps You to Measure Progress*** – You can even practice accountability with someone you know, and you are very close to. This person will help you set the right milestones and also help you define success in the best manner possible. In this way, you can not only keep track of the progress you have made so far but also slowly go close to your goals.

- ***Stay Engaged*** – When you are walking on the path towards your goals, there will be several things that will come to distract you, and all these factors will be ready to take you off your course. There will be times when you don't feel like doing anything or feel bored, but accountability will keep you going towards the finish line.

- ***Make You More Responsible*** – Responsibility is a big factor that helps people in achieving what they want, and when you have someone by your side to help you be accountable for your actions, you will keep pushing until you reach your goal. Slowly and steadily, you will be making progress and you will be successful in eliminating all the excuses.

How to Stay Accountable?

If you want to hold yourself accountable for all the things that you have planned for yourself, it is time that you start doing these things:

Be Honest with Yourself

Everyone has some talent or the other, but there are also ways in which they struggle. Some people might be good at public speaking but alternatively, they might not be good at writing stuff down. That is why goal setting has to be done after giving considerable thought and also ensure that you are accountable for them.

The goals that you set should be sensible so that they focus more on your strengths and less on your weaknesses. So, start by examining yourself properly and be brutally honest during that. You have to clearly assess your shortcomings as well as your strengths. This will help you understand what you are good at and what you are not. Think about the situation when you are going to fall short or when you are going to thrive. There are factors for everyone that help them stay on track. You simply have to identify yours.

Make a Schedule and Commit to It

I often see that people do not have any fixed schedule, and yet they develop deadlines. Having deadlines is good but if you do not have the right schedule that will help you reach that deadline, then it is of no use. When people set goals, they become too much focused on the end result and forget about all those things in between. If you do not have a step-by-step process, achieving any goal can become difficult. You may keep wishing for that success but it is not going to come and step on your doorstep magically if you do not try to make any progress.

One of the most important lessons of goal planning is making a schedule and then staying committed to it without any excuses. In this way, you will have your own game plan in your hands and it will also help you to move towards your finish line persistently and consistently. The objectives that you include in your plan should be time-oriented, and that should be reasonable too. This will ensure that you have your actionable steps ready to fulfill your big goal in life.

For example, let us say that you want to grow your blog and increase your audience than for that, you have to do a series of things like posting content regularly, engaging with your audience, checking insights, and follow through with the procedure every day no matter what comes in your way. Once brand recognition starts happening, you will be moving towards your goal and you will become automatically motivated.

Have Micro-Goals

I think by now, you have your big goal figured out but what you have to do is break it down into micro-goals. When your plan is too overarching, it becomes easier to give in to the thought of procrastination because it feels overwhelming to walk towards your goal. But holding yourself accountable can prevent you from delaying your tasks and one of the ways of doing so is breaking your goal into small segments that you can complete at a time. Whenever you achieve one of these goals, don't forget to celebrate your achievement because that will give you a sense of confidence and motivation to keep moving forward.

Accountability and progress go hand-in-hand. You will not become overwhelmed if you continue taking one step after the other. When you hold yourself accountable, making progress in whatever you are doing becomes a lot easier than before. People stay too focused on the idea of their long-term goals that they often overlook the small wins in life, but at the end of the day, it is these small wins that keep you engaged and moving forward so that one day, you can actually reach your final goal.

Defeat Self-Sabotage

People often have this way of sabotaging their own success in the subconscious minds. This often occurs when you have to step out of your comfort zone, and you cannot handle that. It is basically a type of self-destruction that ultimately leads to dreams being broken and goals shattered. But how will you understand that you have this pattern in yourself as well? Think about any instance when you had all your dreams and micro-goals figured out, but then ultimately, you did not follow through. If it seems familiar, then you have already faced self-sabotaging without even knowing that you were doing it.

So, if you want to hold yourself accountable for the things you are doing so that you can get involved in a more effective goal planning method, then you have to start by figuring out which actions are actually impeding your progress. Once you had identified any such pattern that is affecting you negatively, it will become easier to eliminate them. Everyone has some kind of trigger that sets them on the path of self-sabotage. You have to figure out yours and always be on the lookout for any pattern that you notice in yourself that is causing you to undermine your abilities.

Find an Accountability Partner

I have mentioned this briefly at the beginning of this chapter, but let me explain to you in detail as to who an accountability partner is. Well, it can be anyone who can stay committed to helping you reach your goals. Sometimes, people are working on their own to reach their goal; that is, there is no manager or boos to keep you on track or ensure that you are doing your work on time. In those cases, it is very easy to go off the track but if you can find someone who will be your partner so that you start being answerable to them whenever you fail to do something, following through your goals and actions will become easier.

For example, if you are trying to set up your own online business, then there is no one to look after what you are doing, and in that case, you have only you. But if you find a partner, then reaching milestones can be made easier. But whoever this partner is, make sure that he/she gives you completely unbiased feedback; otherwise, the process is not going to work.

Celebrate Every Win

One of the most important steps of being accountable is celebrating your wins, no matter how small they are. Take some time out to celebrate what you have achieved because, after all the hard work, you deserve a pat on your back. This will not only help you to stay more focused but also give you a momentum to work harder. Every win that you have is like reinforcement towards achieving bigger goals.

By celebrating, I do not mean making grand gestures. It can be something very small like treating yourself to some food you like or watching one episode of your favorite series. Whatever you treat yourself with must be meaningful to you so that after you do it, you feel energized.

Also, after the week is over, write down all your successes in the form of a list and then hang that list somewhere you can see it, and it is always in front of your eyes. Whenever you achieve something else, add it to that list. This is nothing but a boost to your confidence. You can even share your small wins on social media if it is something you want to do. Do whatever you want to make yourself feel good and accomplished.

Chapter 4: Step 4 – Create a Timeline

When you are trying to practice effective goal setting, creating a timeline is probably one of the most important steps; otherwise, you can even take forever to achieve one goal and that is not a practical way to do it. Whether you are trying to achieve your small goals or the big ones, having a timeline is important. But these deadlines cannot be arbitrary; otherwise, success will remain a far-fetched concept.

You have to choose your timeline strategically so that with each day that you work, you move closer to the goal that you have. This will also help you realize small wins at certain intervals, and this is very important if you want to keep moving forward. But if you set a timeline in such a way that you are having a hectic day on all days in a week, working like a maniac, then that is not going to help your cause. It is only going to make you anxious and stressed. Moreover, the end results will also suffer in quality and so deadlines are a double-edges sword. You have to implement them in the right way; otherwise, everything can go wrong very easily. That is a fallacy that you have to face as a result of negative planning but there are so many advantages of setting a timeline that you cannot ignore.

Benefits of Setting a Timeline

Here are some benefits that you are going to enjoy once you learn how to create a suitable timeline:

Encourages Accountability

When you are setting a deadline for your work, you are actually putting a purpose in your life that you have to complete a certain task within a certain period of time. Whether that deadline has been set by you or by anyone else like your boss, what matters is that all of you are working towards a common goal.

Also, when you are imposing deadlines on yourself, you are being responsible to yourself to meet those deadlines. It automatically encourages you to be responsible for whatever the outcome is.

Gives You Momentum in the Right Direction

Sometimes, people are not able to achieve what they wanted even when their goal planning was promising because they were not moving in the right direction or they lacked the momentum to do so. But with the help of strategic deadlines, you can ensure that you are moving in the right direction at all times. Yes, at first, you might not be that much comfortable working within a timeline but with time, you will become better at it and you will see how it gives you more confidence.

Moreover, when you have a deadline, you have to complete that task within that time period, and so when you take a step in the right direction, you become closer to your ultimate goal. The incremental progression for every person is different and the pace is never the same. But no matter what your pace is, it is important that you do not lose this momentum.

Encourage Creativity and Innovation

Every successful person has admitted this that whenever they are working on a timeline, they become more engaged in the work, and that is how they also generate a lot of value. When used in the right manner, deadlines can actually help you strive towards excellence. It can be something like completing your client's work way before the deadline for submitting the project and exceeding everyone's expectations.

When you have to finish a job within a selected period of time, you have to bring forth your best management skills and creativity, and this is how you achieve your goals.

How to Set an Effective Timeline?

If your timeline has not been created with considerable thought, then it will do you more bad than good. It can even hold you back from achieving your full potential. If the timeline is unrealistic, then you will not only fail to meet it but also lose your self-esteem by giving in to procrastination. But if you want to ensure positive results, then here are some steps that we are going to discuss in this section and once you go through them, you are going to take your goal-setting skills to the next level.

When you are making a timeline for your project, you are actually breaking it down chronologically so that it becomes easier for you to complete it without becoming overwhelmed. Also, a single glance at your timeline will make you aligned with it and give you all the information you need. Your entire goal or the tasks at hand will be shaped by your timeline, and it will give you a planned way to visualize all that you want to accomplish. But creating a timeline is not everything. You also have to learn to manage it efficiently as well. Similarly, if the timeline that you have created is not good, then your entire project will be in a mess and your clients will be unhappy.

Understand the Full Scope of Your Project

No matter what the size of your project is, there should always be a brief. The brief serves as a foundation for your project, and if you want the outcome to be good, these foundations will have to be maintained properly. The brief will also give you a proper understanding of the requirements of your project. Creating a brief sometimes also requires you to consult with your client closely and it can take some time too but you should do this task with extreme care and precision because it is going to be the steering wheel of your entire task.

Divide the Goal into Small Parts

In Chapter 3, I already spoke about setting micro-goals, but in this section, I am going to speak about it with respect to setting a timeline. Getting things done can be pretty easy if you think about it that way. When you have a brief of your work in hand, you already know how the big picture looks like. Now, all you need to do is zoom into that big picture to find the smaller parts. There is a term that is used to refer to this – WBS or Work Breakdown Structure. This is when you are creating smaller deliverables from your entire work and you can call each of those small deliverables as work packages.

Now, let us say, you are building a website for your client and that means there is a lot of work to do and each work package would then include – finding a proper theme for the design of the website, a proper plan of content, making that content, fixing SEO, and so on. The scope statement is what will determine what these small work packages will look like.

Find Out What the Dependencies Are

Every project always has some tasks that cannot be done on their own because they depend on certain other tasks. For example, you will not be able to create the content for your client's website if the content plan is not ready yet. In simpler terms, there is a natural order for some of the tasks in a project. And if your project is quite complex, then the number of such dependencies in it is bound to increase. So, you have to start organizing everything and decide which of the tasks have to be completed before others so that the process can go on smoothly.

One of the easier ways to separate these dependencies is that you can color-code them after writing all the tasks on a piece of paper.

Figure Out How Much Time Will Be Needed for Each Task

Now that the organization part is done, you have to find the estimated time that will be required for completing each of these tasks. Some tasks might require only a couple of days, while some of them might require two weeks.

In this way, you have to start spacing out all these tasks on a horizontal line, and soon, you will have the total time that will be required to complete one project. But I must warn you, assumptions about the time required are not always going to turn out as accurate but you have to do your best to make them accurate. If you need help, then consult other members on your team so that each of them can provide their input as to how long they need to complete the task.

Measure Your Resource Availability

Resources are not in abundance. In fact, they are often limited, whether you are talking about technology, money, or manpower. So, before finalizing the timeline, you also have to take into account the resources you have. For example, a team member might be an expert in one of the tasks and thus, that will be completed in no time but on the other hand, another task might be new to all of you and in that case, it will take more time. Also, you cannot keep working 24/7 so you also have limited time in a day to work on the project. Your timeline should be taking all of these factors into account.

Create Milestones

Yes, you have divided the project into small parts, but sometimes, it can get overwhelming if you don't fix milestones for your project. These should certain major points in your project and when you pass them, you'll know that your project is in good health and going in the right direction. It also comes in handy when you have to let the stakeholders know about your progress.

Build Your Timeframe

Now, this is the fun part. All the tasks have to be set in proper chronological order, and the framework should be easily understandable and adaptable. And add the milestones right in the end which will finally polish things off.

Chapter 5: Step 5 – Create an Action Plan

Goal planning is not only about setting goals but also having a properly laid out action plan to achieve those goals. Your goals are there to give you a purpose in life, and have you ever thought about how you are going to move forward if you did not have a clear plan of action? The lack of a proper plan is also why so many people fail to keep moving forward. Nothing is going to work if your plan is not good and so in this chapter, I am going to tell you about how you can make an action plan for your goals.

Your Goals Should Be SMART

I think most of you have heard about SMART goals. It is basically an acronym used to describe how your goals should be. When it comes to business management and goal setting, SMART goal planning is very popular and here is what the term means –

- *S For Specific* – As I told you before in this guide, your goals cannot be vague, and you have to be very clear about what it is that you really want. That is why you need to start questioning yourself as to what you want and why you want it.

- *M For Measurable* – The progress to your goal should be measurable, and that is why you should engage tangible metrics for it. In simpler terms, your goal has to be quantified. If you are planning to earn more money, you have to define your more and label it with a specific amount that you have in mind.

- *A For Attainable* – Yes, you should challenge yourself now and then by stretching your goals but don't stretch them so much that they become unattainable. When your goals become impossible to attain, you are only setting yourself up for frustration.

- *R For Relevant* – Your goal should be properly aligned with what you ultimately want in life. Once you start questioning yourself about how much the goal matters to you, you will be able to figure out the objective of your goal and also come to know whether it will be productive to pursue it or not.

- *T For Time* – No matter what your goal is, setting a deadline for it is what is important. It can be a monthly target or even a weekly one. Whatever it is, when you have a deadline, it becomes easier to stay on track and take action now.

Proceed One Step at a Time

Your plan is most likely to falter if you try to do too many things at a time. That is why it is important that you take only one step at a time. Moreover, the more things you handle at a time, the more it will become chaotic. Seeking clarity should be of utmost priority in goal planning. Your goals usually revolve around several aspects of your life and not just your work. You have goals that are regarding your personal relationships, and then you have goals for your finances too. Stop letting fear occupy your mind and take a small at a time towards what you want. If you think about all the things at a time, you will see that there are lots of steps to be taken, but once you start, it will gradually become less overwhelming.

Learn to Prioritize

Prioritizing your goals is a very important skill that everyone needs to learn. More often than not, people keep delaying walking towards their goals because they don't know where to start. That is why you have to learn how to prioritize and figure out what you want to do now and what can be done later on. Don't always give in to the temptation of multitasking. You cannot really watch Netflix and complete that task at the same time without running the quality of the outcome.

The human mind can remember only so much, and so you should take the help of online calendars or apps that will remind you when you have to submit what. You can set reminders for every step of the way so that you don't forget anything.

Inculcate the Right Habits

Your daily habits play a very big role in helping you to reach your ultimate goal. If you don't start aligning your habits towards your goal, it can become really challenging to achieve what you want. For example, if your goal is to lose a certain amount of weight by the end of the month, and yet you end up eating burgers every day, it is not going to help you in any way. You have to start eating nutritious foods so that you can become more aligned with your weight loss goal.

Now, the same thing applies to goals that are career oriented. If you want to get more clients for your business, you will have to start networking, but instead of that, if you choose to cow away from community meetings or gatherings, then you cannot reach your goal. I am not saying that transforming yourself is going to be easy but it is something that you have to be willing to do if you truly want to achieve things in life.

Determine the Actions and Make a Schedule

You have to figure out the steps that lead to your goals, that is, your micro-goals. Once that is done, think about what actions you will have to take in order to reach your goals. When you complete this step, you will have all that you need to make a schedule. You need to have a daily plan ready at your disposal that you can follow and slowly become closer to your goal. A schedule will also help you to make the best use of the time that is available to you. You will get to see where you are losing time and where you can do something for efficient time utilization.

There is another thing that you should remember, and getting things done does not mean that you are going to cram up your schedule with work and only work. You have to leave some time out for your family as well and some time for your own self. This will keep your mind refreshed and you will be even more motivated towards work. This is how motivational psychology works.

Follow Through

Once you have your daily plan in place, all you have to do is follow it diligently. Even if you have everything you need to achieve your goals, you need to follow the plan; otherwise, you are not going to get the results you want. Check your to-do list daily and see what things need completion. There will be times when you will feel as if nothing is going the right way and it is completely normal to feel demotivated but you simply have to figure out your own ways in which you can keep going towards your goal. Yes, I know what you might be thinking that this is a no-brainer but astonishingly, most people struggle with this. There are so many people who cannot keep doing what they are doing consistently and so they give up.

One of the things that you can do to motivate yourself is to keep track of all that you have achieved and this will give you a sense of self-confidence and make you want to do more work.

Remind yourself every day, and once you have your goals in place, you are not going to achieve them overnight. It is a process and it requires time and patience. Whether you are trying to learn a new skill or whether you are trying to lose weight, no matter what you try to do, an action plan is necessary because it will give you the direction and all you need to do is follow.

If you are finding it difficult to stay focused on your plan, then you can write things down. Many people find it easier to achieve things when they have it written down. It increases visibility and clarity and once you have written down what you need to do, hang that list on the wall in front of your work desk or anywhere where you will be able to see it frequently, especially when you are working. Also, you need to keep reviewing and reassessing your action plans because there might be some changes based on circumstances. Never blame others when something is not going the way you wanted it to. It is you who has to take responsibility for your actions. If you are consistent enough, you will reach your goals.

There might be times when you went off the track with your goals but you have to maintain resiliency. You have to pick yourself up and again come back on track. If you find it difficult to get back up, remind yourself of all the hard work that you have put it. So, why back out now? Your vision should always be with you so that you never lose sight of what you want.

Chapter 6: Step 6 – Assess Your Progress

How much revenue increase have you seen this month? How much weight have you lost since you started hitting the gym? Most people will not have specific answers to such progress-based questions because they don't keep track. It is true that assessing your progress is a lot of work, but it is highly beneficial in getting things done.

Why Should You Assess Your Progress?

It is important to assess how much progress you are making with each passing day and in fact, people who do this are more likely to fulfill their dreams and aspirations than those who don't do it. Here are some of the benefits of assessing your progress that you should know about –

- *Measurement Effect* – The moment you start measuring your progress, you will see that you have this urge to do more and keep moving forward. This is called the measurement effect. For example, when you want to save money, you start keeping track of how much money you are spending on eating out and you automatically stop spending so much. Similarly, when you think that you are not drinking enough water every day, you start tracking the number of glasses of water and in this way, you end up drinking more. This is basically nothing but human nature and it happens to everyone.

- *Helps Determining a Baseline* – When you assess your progress or keep track of it, you also can figure out what your baseline is. For example, if you are taking 1 hour to do something, then you should set a target of 30 minutes instead of 15 minutes; otherwise, it would be quite unrealistic.

- *Reminds You How Far You Came* – When you know where you are currently at, that is your baseline, you also can see how far you have come. In short, when your wins are in front of you, staying motivated towards your ultimate goal becomes way easier. It will also help in maintaining your confidence levels.

- *Identify Your Problems* – There is another benefit of assessing your progress, and that is – you can easily figure out what your problems are or what is acting as a barrier in your path. In case you are not making any progress for the past few weeks, you will come to know of it only if you assess it from time to time.

- *Helps in Enhancing Your Attention* – You can carry on with your plan only when you are paying attention to your goals. Assessing your progress is a personal choice that you have to make, but when you willingly make that choice and start focusing on the little things, you become more attentive towards your work. Moreover, this same behavior will also help you in prioritizing your work. Although assessment of your progress might seem a bit difficult at first, with the guide that I am going to provide you in this chapter, it will become way easier.

How to Assess Your Progress?

There are several ways in which you can assess and keep track of the progress that you are making. Making this assessment will ensure that your goals are in line with your ultimate motive and inner goal. With time, you will see that you have become more purposeful and you are making more progress than ever before.

If you don't know where to start, follow this guide:

Practice Quantitative Measurement

If you are performing an assessment of your goals for the first time, then I would say that you should start with quantitative measurement mostly because it is much easier than the qualitative process. There are different methods that can be followed in order to quantify your progress. For example, let us consider that you are trying to lose weight and control your appetite. In that case, you can measure your progress by seeing how many pounds you have lost in a certain duration of time. In some cases, you will that there several ways in which you can measure your progress, and you have to stick with the process that suits you best.

Follow the Seinfeld Method

This method has been named after comedian Jerry Seinfeld because he was the one who came up with this method in the first place. The main idea behind this method is to promote a constant state of improvement in you and trust me; most of you are going to love this method. It can be used whenever you are trying to make some progress towards your ultimate goal or if you are trying to build any daily habit. Here is how you are going to follow this process –

- Start with a calendar where you will list your daily goals against each day, and then whenever that day is completed and you have fulfilled your goals, you are going to check it off.

- You have to continue doing this on a daily basis, and very soon, you will be looking at a calendar where all the days have been checked off.

- And most importantly, vow to you yourself that you are not going to break this chain no matter what.

That is all this process is truly about. After a certain point of time, you will see that you have ticked off 20 days successively and it forms a chain, and you will not break the chain because you'll know that if you do that, you will have to start again at zero and build the chain all over again.

Start Every Day at Zero

In the previous method, you saw how maintaining goals for each day and then checking them off the list can help you move forward. There is another thing that you should know in this respect. When you are starting your project, your finish line will be quite definite and clear to you. The more you get closer to the end; it might seem blurry. This is because you have been putting your effort for so many days and now you want to see results but you still have to go all the way until the end for results. And that is why the middle zone is the toughest and that is where most people back down. But you should not do that.

Once you have found the right direction and motivation, make sure you begin each day of work with a clean slate. This means that you should not allow the work to accumulate and complete each day's work on that day itself. When you do that, you are able to start the new day with a much better sense of accomplishment, increased focus and you will want to move forward with even more vigor. But make sure you are forming daily quotas that are small and not too huge to handle. When the quota is small, it will be easier for you to complete it and move on to the next step.

Maintain a Journal

Maintaining a journal and writing in it for at least 5 minutes in a day is also one of the effective strategies for assessing your success. Your journal will basically act as a record of your progress, and you have to update it every day. You should also add some of your personal notes which are mainly going to be your personal thoughts on various subjects and how you think you can improve. You should also write about any problem that might crop up along the path. In case you did not meet your target of the day for some reason, you have to figure out the reason behind it and then write it down in your journal. This will help you overcome a similar situation in the future. Then, figuring out the best course of action will become way easier for you.

Your journal will be a reference for you whenever something goes wrong and you can refer to it for solutions. Moreover, apart from the negatives, you should note down anything positive that happens so that it can motivate you to work better. Getting things done will only be like you planned when you learn to appreciate your wins and learn from your failures. If you want the best out of this exercise, then you should not depend on your digital modes of writing but turn to a pen and paper. Some people maintain a journal on their laptop but that is not going to be as fruitful as writing down in a journal. And when you look at your journal at the end of the month, you will no longer feel overwhelmed. In fact, you will feel satisfied with how far you have come.

Perform a Monthly Personal Review

Performing a monthly review of the work you have done so far is truly one of the best ways of measuring your progress. It is like conducting a meeting with yourself once in every month. And then you have to keep doing the same process month after month. The meeting should not be deferred and make it a non-negotiable event of your life. In case something very important arises, and you have to reschedule your personal meeting, do it but never try to cancel it otherwise, you will be doing yourself more harm than good.

Some of the things that you can track during such personal reviews are:

- Things that you have accomplished and proud of
- Any notes that you have taken on anything new that you tried
- A progress report on anything that you started doing for the first time
- Any personal goal or long-term goal that you are working towards
- Anything that you want to particularly focus on in the upcoming month and any particular goal that you want to achieve

In the first month, completing this review might take some effort and time but with the following months, it will become easier. The review must be short and concise. Don't stretch it too much.

Chapter 7: Step 7 – Reward Yourself

In this chapter, we are going to discuss the last step of goal planning, which roots from motivational psychology, and it is about rewarding yourself. Whenever you have accomplished some goal or completed a task, you need to reward yourself in some manner. Do you know why? It is because it fills your brain with all sorts of positive emotions and if you keep doing this over and over again, your brain will be linking accomplishments with a sense of pleasure and will be even more motivated to complete tasks on time.

Benefits of Rewarding Yourself

Some people might tell you that rewarding yourself is sort of a frivolous thing to do, but it is nothing like that. When you are working hard to achieve something and even inculcating some new habit, it is important that you treat yourself to something good after achieving results. Doing hard work can be draining and whenever you treat yourself to things you love, you will instantly feel energized and more motivated. It will also help you to continue with your healthy habits without breaking the chain. For better understanding, here are some of the benefits that you are going to get if you reward yourself.

Brings Self-Reliance

When you reward yourself, it instantly brings about a feeling of independence from the emotional point of view. This is because you are no longer relying on any external sources for validation, motivation, or any kind of incentive. You simply trust yourself and become more self-reliant by the day. Developing this quality is not easy, especially because ever since childhood, we are taught to depend on something or else.

When you are becoming self-reliant, it means that you have assumed full responsibility for your actions, which is also a direct result of becoming focused on your goals and being successful. So, all of this is basically interconnected. You also become more and more informed about everything that is going on in your surroundings and you don't get influenced by others' comments. Even if someone comes and tries to hurt your self-confidence, you are not dependent on that person for anything and so it shouldn't affect you.

Boosts Self-Esteem

You will come across so many people in your day-to-day life whose main goal is to pull you down and hurt your self-esteem. And if you let each and every one of them affect you, then you are not going to reach your goals. So, let people remind you of your shortcomings, you can avoid being affected by them by rewarding yourself every time you achieve something from your daily goals. Your success will become a far-fetched concept; the more try to dwell on your failure. When your self-esteem is renewed, you will feel even better at work and you will be working harder than ever before. There is no benefit in languishing in self-doubt because you can make mountains move if you put in the effort.

Start Thinking Positively

One of the major hurdles that everyone has to cross on their way to their ultimate goal is their own negative thoughts. On the other hand, rewarding your wins no matter how small they are, brings about a positive vibe and feeling, and the benefits of that are endless. If you cannot think positively, you will not be able to reach your personal heights. But rewarding yourself and celebrating your successes will give you a boost and make you think positively.

Become More Energized

This is something that we can all agree on. When you are doing work for a long time, it can at times, get monotonous, but once you achieve a goal and reward yourself, you are able to break that monotony. If you keep doing your work for hours without doing anything else in between your work will seem boring to you after a certain period of time and that is why a shift in perspective becomes all the more important. When you are rewarding yourself, you are actually rebooting your system and doing something else for a while that you love or something that makes you happy even if it means treating yourself to your favorite cupcake.

How to Reward Yourself?

If you have been working for a long time and not rewarding yourself for all the amazing achievements, then it is time you take a break and do that because you completely deserve it. And in case you are out of ideas as to how you can reward yourself, here are some of the ways in which you can do so.

Plan a Movie Night

Is there a new movie releasing that you had been dying to watch? Then, get the tickets right away. Finish your work early to get tickets for the night show. But if you are not feeling like going outside, then you can also plan a movie night at your home. Moreover, you get to see the film of your choice and that too in pajamas.

Take Yourself Out to a Nice Restaurant or Café

If food is something you love and that comes to your mind as the first thing when we are talking about rewards, then why not take yourself out to a place that you always wanted to go? If you cannot go there during office hours, then you can order takeout, or you can go there for breakfast or dinner, whichever suits your schedule. There is nothing more sumptuous than enjoying a good meal after you have achieved one of your goals.

Read a Book

If you are looking for an option that you can practice in between work, then I would say reading a book is the best you have. If you have two to three goals to achieve in a day and you have already achieved the first one, then give yourself a 15 minutes break and read a few pages from your favorite book. In this way, your mind will be refreshed and you will be working with even more vigor so that you can complete your next task and move on to another chapter in the book.

Go Shopping

If you are a person who loves shopping, then you can do that too. Whatever you buy, it doesn't have to be expensive. You can buy a new top or a pair of shoes or even sunglasses. You can even buy accessories. Buy whatever you feel you like but make sure it is in your budget. If you want something that requires a bigger investment, then you can set a monthly goal and when you achieve it, you can spend some money on buying the dress that you always wanted.

Make Some Desserts

If you are working from home and you love cooking, then why not try baking some of your favorite desserts or maybe try to bake something new! Baking can be therapeutic for those who love to do it. And then you will have some treats for yourself. You can also prepare any other type of food item as well.

Enjoy a Bubble Bath

You can even reward yourself with a bubble bath or a long shower once your goal of the day is achieved. This will make you feel fresh and revived. It will also take away all the tension and stress of the day.

Get a Manicure

You can get a manicure or even a spa. The point is not what you get but treating yourself to some service in a parlor if that is what you want.

Go on a Vacation

After you have achieved one of the major goals, you can even plan a vacation for yourself. Yes, I know that going on a vacation is not something you can do every week, but it can be something that you can do a few times in a year. So, you can save money accordingly that you will be rewarding yourself the type of vacation you like when you have met your quarterly goals.

Tips for Rewarding Yourself

If you want to establish a proper routine and start getting things done, then you have to establish a proper self-rewarding system and here are some tips for you –

- Firstly, you have to ensure that your system is effective. Everyone has his/her own interests. So, you have to take into consideration what your interests are before you decide the reward. Whatever reward suits someone else might not suit you, so irrespective of the ideas that I gave in the previous section, you have to look within yourself and ask yourself what you want.

- The next thing to keep in mind is that there should not be a direct substitute for your reward system, meaning that you have to establish the fact in your mind that you will only get the reward when you work hard for it. Also, if you notice that your emotions are not changing even when you are rewarding yourself, then you have to know that you have chosen the wrong reward and it's time you rethink.

- Don't go out of proportion with the reward. If you have completed only one micro-goal out of four that you have on any particular day, then you should not just go and gift yourself an expensive coat. If you have completed a very tough task, then you can reward yourself something bigger, but if the task was small, then stick to something more affordable and smaller yet meaningful.

- Your reward should not be something that is harmful to your progress. For example, if your goal is to start clean eating and for the first step that you have accomplished, you reward yourself with a packet of chips, then that is not the kind of reward that I am talking about because it will only harm the progress that you have made. It is not going to make things better, but only worse.

Rewarding yourself is a part of the goal-setting process, and there are no hard and fast rules for them but you should still be sensible about what rewards you are giving yourself.

Conclusion

Thank you for making it through to the end of *"How to Set Goals"*, let's hope it was informative and able to provide you with all of the tools you need to achieve your goals whatever they may be.

In this guide, I have shown you how goals are important for every aspect of your life and what effective goal setting looks like. It is true that achieving your goals is not always as you think it would be, but you can make your chances of attaining your goals better by implementing effective goal planning techniques which we have already discussed. Successful goal setting is an art and if you do not have direction or focus, it is not going to work out. But since you have reached this point, it means that you have already been through the entire guide. I am glad that you chose to take goal setting seriously and now it is time that you start implementing the strategies in your own life as well.

To make the process easier, I outlined seven steps so that people do not have a problem in understanding what they have to do at every step of the way. So, think about the goal that you have in life, picture it in your head and visualize that you have already achieved it. Does that feel good? I bet it does, and you can make it all come true only if you start following the things mentioned in this guide. The road to success is not going to be easy but it is not impossible too. The speed at which you will reach your goal might not be the same as someone else and so you should never compare your journey to someone else's. Just stick to your action plan and your dreams are definitely going to come true.

More by Miles Toole

Discover all books from the Personal Productivity Series by Miles Toole at:

bit.ly/miles-toole

Book 1: *How to Be Productive*

Book 2: *How to Manage Time*

Book 3: *How to Be Organized*

Book 4: *How to Stay Focused*

Book 5: *How to Set Goals*

Book 6: *How to Stop Procrastinating*

Book 7: *How to Change Habits*

Book 8: *How to Stay Motivated*

Themed book bundles available at discounted prices:

bit.ly/miles-toole

Made in United States
North Haven, CT
16 January 2024

47567321R00035